HAL•LEONARD
INSTRUMENTAL
PLAY-ALONG

AUDIO
ACCESS
INCLUDED

PLAYBACK+
Speed • Pitch • Balance • Loop

PEACEFUL HYMNS

Audio arrangements by Peter Deneff

To access audio visit:
www.halleonard.com/mylibrary
Enter Code
5446-9311-9345-3844

ISBN 978-1-70513-799-4

HAL•LEONARD®

Visit Hal Leonard Online at
www.halleonard.com

Contact us:
Hal Leonard
7777 West Bluemound Road
Milwaukee, WI 53213
Email: info@halleonard.com

In Europe, contact:
Hal Leonard Europe Limited
42 Wigmore Street
Marylebone, London, W1U 2RN
Email: info@halleonardeurope.com

In Australia, contact:
Hal Leonard Australia Pty. Ltd.
4 Lentara Court
Cheltenham, Victoria, 3192 Australia
Email: info@halleonard.com.au

T0057204

ABIDE WITH ME

CELLO

Music by WILLIAM H. MONK

ALL CREATURES OF OUR GOD AND KING

CELLO

Music from *Geistliche Kirchengesang*

ALL HAIL THE POWER OF JESUS' NAME

CELLO

Music by OLIVER HOLDEN

ALL THROUGH THE NIGHT

CELLO

Welsh Folksong

AMAZING GRACE

CELLO

Traditional American Melody

BE THOU MY VISION

CELLO

Traditional Irish

BLESSED ASSURANCE

CELLO

Music by PHOEBE PALMER KNAPP

COME, THOU FOUNT OF EVERY BLESSING

CELLO

Music from John Wyeth's *Repository of Sacred Music*

FAIREST LORD JESUS

CELLO

Music from *Schlesische Volkslieder*

FOR THE BEAUTY OF THE EARTH

CELLO

Music by CONRAD KOCHER

GREAT IS THY FAITHFULNESS

CELLO

Music by WILLIAM M. RUNYAN

HOLY, HOLY, HOLY

CELLO

Music by JOHN B. DYKES

HOW FIRM A FOUNDATION

CELLO

Traditional music compiled by JOSEPH FUNK

I NEED THEE EVERY HOUR

CELLO

Music by ROBERT LOWRY

IT IS WELL WITH MY SOUL

CELLO

Music by PHILIP P. BLISS

JUST AS I AM

CELLO

Music by WILLIAM B. BRADBURY

THE KING OF LOVE MY SHEPHERD IS

CELLO

Traditional Irish Melody

LET ALL MORTAL FLESH KEEP SILENCE

CELLO

17th Century French Carol

MY FAITH LOOKS UP TO THEE

CELLO

Music by LOWELL MASON

NEARER, MY GOD, TO THEE

CELLO

Music by LOWELL MASON

WERE YOU THERE WHEN THEY CRUCIFIED MY LORD?

CELLO

Traditional

WHAT A FRIEND WE HAVE IN JESUS

CELLO

Music by CHARLES C. CONVERSE

WONDROUS LOVE

CELLO

Southern American Folk Hymn